A Note to Parents

Eyewitness Readers is a compelling new program for beginning readers, designed in conjunction with leading literacy experts, including Dr. Linda Gambrell, President of the National Reading Conference and past board member of the International Reading Association.

Eyewitness has become the most trusted name in illustrated books, and this new series combines the highly visual *Eyewitness* approach with engaging, easy-to-read stories. Each *Eyewitness Reader* is guaranteed to capture a child's interest while developing his or her reading skills, general knowledge, and love of reading.

The four levels of *Eyewitness Readers* are aimed at different reading abilities, enabling you to choose the books that are exactly right for your children:

Level 1, for **Preschool to Grade 1**
Level 2, for **Grades 1 to 3**
Level 3, for **Grades 2 and 3**
Level 4, for **Grades 2 to 4**

The "normal" age at which a child begins to read can be anywhere from three to eight years old, so these levels are intended only as a general guideline.

No matter which level you select, you can be sure that you are helping your child learn to read, then read to learn!

A DK PUBLISHING BOOK
www.dk.com

Created by Leapfrog Press Ltd

Project Editor Naia Bray-Moffatt
Art Editor Andrew Burgess
Photography John Daniels

For Dorling Kindersley
Senior Editor Linda Esposito
Managing Art Editor Peter Bailey
US Editor Regina Kahney
Production Josie Alabaster

Reading Consultant
Linda B. Gambrell, Ph.D.

First American Edition, 1999
2 4 6 8 10 9 7 5 3 1
Published in the United States by
DK Publishing, Inc.
95 Madison Avenue, New York, New York 10016

Published in Great Britain by Dorling Kindersley Limited.

Library of Congress Cataloging-in-Publication Data
Hodge, Judith 1963-
  Animal hospital / by Judith Hodge -- 1st American ed.
    p.   cm. -- (Eyewitness readers. Level 2)
  Summary: Two children find an injured duck, take it to a
veterinarian at an animal hospital, and watch as she cares for it.
  ISBN 0-7894-3996-4 (pb) ISBN 0-7894-3997-2 (hc)
  1.Veterinary hospitals--Juvenile literature. [1. Veterinary hospitals.
2. Veterinarians. 3. Ducks.] I. Title. II. Series.
  SF604.55.H63   1999
  636.089--dc21
                                            98-41847
                                               CIP
                                                AC

Color reproduction by Colourscan, Singapore
Printed and bound in Belgium by Proost

The publisher would like to thank the following:
Additional design: Jane Horne
Models: Rachel Walker, Andrew Burgess, Karen Clifford,
Harry and Jack Clifford, Philippa Parsons,
Animal handler: Carolyn Fry
Additional photography by Tracy Morgan, Dave King,
Andreas Einsiedel, Bob Langrish, Ray Moller, Andy Crawford,
Steve Shott and Andrew Burgess.

EYEWITNESS READERS

Level 2
GRADES 1-3

Animal Hospital

Written by Judith Walker-Hodge

BR
WALKER
1999

DK

DK PUBLISHING, INC.
www.dk.com

One day Jack and Luke
were playing near their house
when they heard a strange noise.
They went to see what it was.

"It's a duck," said Luke.

"Its wing looks hurt."

"We shouldn't move it," said Jack.

"Let's get Dad."

Dad got a cardboard box.
He put the duck gently
into the box.
Then the family drove to
the animal hospital.
"Quack! Quack!" said the duck.

quack quack

"Poor thing," said Mom.
"I think she's scared."
"She's just been in a car
with Dad driving!" laughed Jack.

Mallard ducks
The duck in this story
is a female mallard duck.
Male mallard ducks are more colorful.
They have green heads and yellow beaks.

"Hello," said the vet. "I'm Dr. Corby.
What have we got here?"
She took the duck out of the box
and looked at it carefully.

Bird wings
Wing bones are fragile.
They are mostly hollow,
which means they are light.
This makes it easier
for birds to fly.

"She's hurt her wing," said the vet.
"But luckily it isn't broken."

Dr. Corby
strapped the wing
to the bird's body
with a bandage.
"It will take
about three weeks
to heal,"
she told the boys.

Andrew, one of the nurses,
took the duck
to a special area out back.
"All the birds are kept here,"
he said.

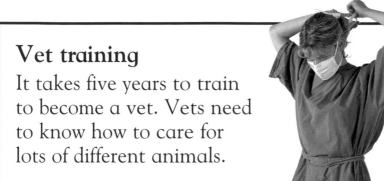

Vet training
It takes five years to train
to become a vet. Vets need
to know how to care for
lots of different animals.

"This is Gertie the goose.
She swallowed a fish hook,
but she's all better now.

Has your duck
got a name?"
"No," said Jack,
"not yet."
"How about Jemima?"
Luke said.
"Yes," Jack nodded.
"Maybe Gertie and
Jemima can be friends!"

The nurse put some pellets
and fresh water on the ground
next to Jemima.
"Can we come and visit her?"
Luke asked.
"Sure," said the nurse.
"Come back
next week."

"Thanks!" said the boys.
They rushed inside
to tell their parents.

Jack's friend Alice was
in the waiting room.
She was holding
a rabbit.
On the floor
beside her
was a basket.

"Look what I've got!" said Alice.
Jack opened the basket
and out jumped five kittens!

"We've brought them for
a check-up," said Alice's mom.
"Can you help carry the kittens
into the vet's room?"

"Hello again," said the vet
as the boys came in.
"They're helping Alice,"
said Alice's mom with a smile.
The vet listened to each kitten's
heart and lungs with her stethoscope.

She looked into
their eyes and ears
and checked
their fur for fleas.

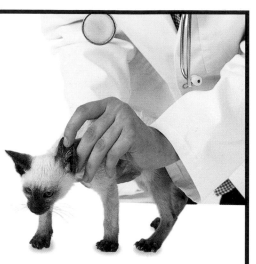

Then she gave each kitten a shot
to protect it against cat flu
and other illnesses.

Caring for cats

Cats need their fur
checked often for fleas.
They need to be checked
for worms too.

Next it was the rabbit's turn.

"He's not eating," Alice told the vet.

Dr. Corby looked inside
the rabbit's mouth.

"I think I know what the problem is,"
she said.

"His teeth are too long – no wonder he can't chew his carrots!"
She clipped the teeth with a pair of special scissors.
"It doesn't hurt him, I promise," she told the children.

Rabbit teeth

A rabbit's teeth never stop growing. That's because in the wild they eat tough plant stems, which wear their teeth down.

quack
quack

The next week, Jack and Luke
went back to the hospital.
Jemima was now waddling around
the yard, quacking happily.

"She can't swim yet because of
the bandage," Dr. Corby told the boys.

"Her webbed feet will crack
if they get too dry.
Would you like to help
sponge them?"
"Yes!" said the boys.
But just then a siren went off.
ring ring ring

The boys followed Dr. Corby
to the animal ambulance.
"What have we got?"
she asked the nurse.
"A dog's been hit by a car,"
said the nurse.
"His front leg
looks broken."

X-rays
These are special photographs taken by invisible rays. The rays pass through the body and show the bones.

"We'll need to take some X-rays right away," said the vet. "Let's get him inside."

Dr. Corby showed the boys the X-rays.

"Look," she pointed.

"Can you see the broken bone?"

Jack and Luke nodded.

"I'll have to fix it by operating.

You two wait outside."

Dr. Corby made sure
everything was clean.
She put on a gown
and a special mask.

Then she scrubbed
her hands.

"The dog
will be fine,"
said the vet
after the
operation.

Two weeks later, Jack and Luke
went back to visit Jemima.
They watched Dr. Corby
take off the bandage
and check Jemima's wing.

"She's ready
to go home,"
said the vet.
"All we
have to do
is find her one."

Just then Andrew came in.
"A corn snake is missing,"
he told the vet.

"Can I help look for it?" asked Luke.
"I love snakes."

"No, no," said Dr. Corby.
"Corn snakes are harmless.
I'm sure it will
turn up."

The next day, Dr. Corby phoned
the boys' home.
"I've found a place for Jemima,"
she told their mother,
"at a farm with a pond.
Can the boys come with me?"
"Of course!" said Mom.

At the farm,
the vet went to
the barn to look
at a horse with
an infected hoof.

The children watched the vet
clean the horse's foot.
Then she gave the animal
a shot to fight
the infection.

"I'm almost done here,"
she said to the boys.
"Why don't you show Jemima
her new home on the pond?"

Horse shoes
Horses wear metal shoes to
protect their feet.
The job of reshoeing horses
is done by a farrier.
Shoes last 4 to 8 weeks.

Lots of ducks were swimming
in the farm pond.
Jack took Jemima out of her box.
Jemima didn't move.
"Go on, Jemima," Jack whispered.
She spread her wings,
then stepped into the pond
and swam off with her new friends.

Dr. Corby was putting
her instruments away in her bag.
"There's something moving in there!"
cried Luke.

Dr. Corby looked inside.
"You found the snake after all!"
laughed the vet.

Animal Gallery

Mallard ducks are wild birds
that live on ponds and rivers.
Some people keep other breeds
of "domestic" or tame ducks
for their eggs.

Cats were first kept as pets in the
Middle East about 4,000 years ago.
Now there are more than 50 million
pet cats in the United States alone.
There are more than 100 official breeds
of pet cat.

Pet rabbits are popular because
they are easy to look after.
There are more than 50 breeds
of rabbit to choose from.

Dogs are loyal pets.
There are more breeds of dog
than any other pet animal:
130 breeds in Britain and about
160 in the United States.

Snakes make unusual pets.
Corn snakes are harmless
but there are over 400 types
of snake that are poisonous.

Horses have been kept by people
as a means of transportation for
over 3,000 years. Today there are
more than 75 million farm horses
and more than 100 different breeds.